IDIOT'S

Pocket Guide to

DOS 6

By Kelly Oliver

alpha
books

A Division of Prentice Hall Computer Publishing
11711 North College Avenue, Carmel, Indiana 46032 USA

International Standard Book Number:1-56761-303-9
Library of Congress Catalog Card Number: 93-71928

95 94 93   8 7 6 5 4 3 2 1

Interpretation of the printing code: the rightmost number of the first series of numbers is the year of the book's printing; the rightmost number of the second series of numbers is the number of the book's printing. For example, a printing code of 93-1 shows that the first printing of the book occurred in 1993.

Screen reproductions in this book were created by means of the program Collage Plus from Inner Media, Inc., Hollis, NH.

Printed in the United States of America

Trademarks

Publisher, Marie Butler-Knight; **Associate Publisher**, Lisa A. Bucki; **Managing Editor**, Elizabeth Keaffaber; **Acquisitions Manager**, Stephen R. Poland; **Development Editor**, Sherry Kinkoph; **Manuscript Editor**, San Dee Phillips; **Cover Designer**, Jean Bisesi; **Designer**, Kevin Spear; **Indexer**, C. Alan Small, **Production Team**; Diana Bigham, Katy Bodenmiller, Tim Cox, Meshell Dinn, Howard Jones, Tom Loveman, Beth Rago, Carrie Roth, Greg Simsic

Contents

Introduction
Your Computer Won't Work Without It

MS-DOS: The "Mother" of Your Computer

When I was little, my sisters and I played a game called "Mother May I" with our neighbors. I can't remember all the rules exactly, but the goal of the game was to be the first one past a line where the "Mother" was standing. The "Mother" would say something like, "Everyone with a blue shirt take four giant steps forward," or something like that. You had to ask "Mother may I?" before you took the steps, or you would have to go back to the starting line. On top of that, when you asked, "Mother may I?" the Mother could tell you yes or no. Basically, the game was kind of rigged. The Mother could choose a person to win and give that person all the good steps.

MS-DOS is like the "Mother" in "Mother May I." Your computer is relatively useless without DOS (*Disk Operating System*) to tell it how to process the information you give it. DOS controls the whole shebang and tells you whether or not you can do the things you want to do. For instance, you might type in a certain command only to have DOS give you an error message like **Bad command or file name**, which means you have to go back to the beginning and start over.

Thinking back, the whole "Mother May I" game was pretty pointless. It was too easy to mess up and have to start all over. The DOS command prompt (the thing that usually looks like **C:>** where you type in commands) is similar in that it is very easy to mess up.

The commands are hard to remember and it's easy to type in the wrong thing. Fortunately, the brilliant people at Microsoft came up with a way to get around the DOS command prompt: the DOS Shell. With it, you can choose commands from menus and answer questions in dialog boxes. It's much easier to use, especially for a beginner.

Now, don't get anxious with all this talk of commands and error messages. DOS really isn't very hard to use. With this book as a guide, you'll soon be a whiz at using DOS. You'll learn about files, directories, the DOS prompt, the DOS Shell, and all sorts of commands.

How to Use This Book

The *Complete Idiot's Pocket Guide to DOS 6.0* is designed to be a friendly, easy-to-use manual for those of us who are short on time but who need to know the basics about using DOS. Each lesson is brief and to the point and is written with a conversational tone so you won't feel like you have to read each sentence twelve times to understand it.

There are special little features like tips and figures that will help you along the way. (Through most of the book, I'll be talking about selecting commands in the DOS Shell, but there are tips scattered around for all you DOS command line users that tell you what the comparable command is.) You can look at the figures to see examples of the way your screen should look when you perform certain commands or follow a set of instructions.

The tips look like this:

If you read one of these babies, you'll find some information that might turn out to be pretty helpful.

Use the following conventions to help you work through the lessons:

On-screen text	Text that appears on-screen appears in **bold**.
Menu, dialog box, and window names	The first letter of each menu, dialog box, or window name is capitalized.
What you type	The information you type is **bold**.
What you press	The keys you press (for key combinations or commands) appear in **bold**.
Selection letters	The selection letter of each command or option is **bold** (such as File).

You can read the lessons in this book from start to finish, or you can skip around from lesson to lesson. Use this book however you feel most comfortable.

Acknowledgments

I'd like to thank the author of *The 10 Minute Guide to DOS 6.0* and *The Complete Idiot's Guide to DOS*, Jennifer Flynn, for being a good sport and tackling DOS before I had to. Special thanks go to Joe Kraynak, who unknowingly taught me everything I know about DOS. And to Lisa Bucki, Steve Poland, Sherry Kinkoph, and San Dee Phillips, extraordinary editors and direction-givers, many thanks.

Dedication

For Kyle Passon— "the one that makes me laugh."

Lesson 1

What Is This DOS Thing?

First Things First: Start Your PC

A good place to begin learning about DOS is at the beginning: starting your PC. The process of starting a computer is called *booting*. (Oddly enough, this reference to footwear means that the computer "pulls itself up by its bootstraps," so to speak.) When your PC boots, the *disk operating system* (*DOS*) is loaded (copied) into memory. *Memory* is the working area of your PC, where the computer temporarily stores information it needs.

You can load DOS from a *hard disk* or from a *diskette*. (Your hard disk is permanently stored in your computer and is usually drive C. A diskette is a portable floppy disk that you can insert and remove from a floppy disk drive.) If you've already installed DOS on your hard disk, just flip the computer's **ON** switch, and turn on the monitor. If your PC does not have a hard disk or does not have DOS installed yet, put a *system disk* in drive A and turn on the computer. The system disk is the one that contains the operating system's files. You'll use the MS-DOS 6 Startup/Support Diskette here.

Always Be Prepared Like a good scout, you should be prepared for emergencies. That's why you should always make copies of your installation disks (especially if you use them to start your computer every day).

Once your PC is started, it may stop and ask you to verify the current date and time, like a passerby on the street. (If your PC has an internal clock, as most do, you may not see these prompts.) Although this might seem insignificant, it's important that your system uses the correct date and time, because that's how DOS keeps track of changes. If you see the prompt

Current date is 01-01-94
Enter new date:

enter the current date (after the colon) in one of three formats, then press Enter. You can use:

02-20-94
02/20/94
02.20.94

If you see the prompt

Current time is 00:00:01
Enter new time:

enter the current time (after the colon) using 24-hour military time. (Apparently, all computers served in the armed forces.) For example, to enter 2:12 p.m., type **14:12** and press **Enter**. You can also enter the seconds, as in **14:12:33**.

I Started My PC, Now Tell Me What DOS Is

DOS stands for *disk operating system*, which means that DOS is responsible for the operation of your computer (did you think you were responsible?). For example, a program may tell DOS to read the contents of a file, and DOS takes care of the details. (You'll learn more about files in Lesson 2.) DOS is kind of like a sergeant who carries out your commands, doing all the detail work. Of course, that would make you the general.

There are two ways you can give commands to DOS 6: the *DOS command line* and the *DOS Shell*. When you use the DOS command line, you type in a string of characters at the *DOS prompt*. The DOS prompt looks something like C> or C:\>.

You enter the command after the greater-than sign (>), as shown in Figure 1.1. For example, the MEM command tells DOS to report how much available memory it has.

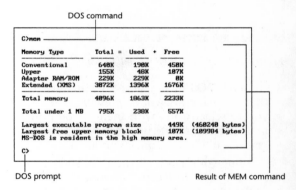

DOS command

```
C>mem

Memory Type       Total =  Used  +  Free

Conventional       640K     190K     450K
Upper              155K      48K     107K
Adapter RAM/ROM    229K     229K       0K
Extended (XMS)    3072K    1396K    1676K

Total memory      4096K    1863K    2233K

Total under 1 MB   795K     238K     557K

Largest executable program size      449K  (460240 bytes)
Largest free upper memory block      107K  (109984 bytes)
MS-DOS is resident in the high memory area.

C>
```

DOS prompt   Result of MEM command

Figure 1.1   Entering commands at the DOS prompt.

After you type the command, press the **Enter** key; DOS then performs the command. (When you press **Enter** after typing **MEM**, a report telling you how much memory your computer has available appears on the monitor.)

You can also issue commands from the DOS Shell. The DOS Shell, shown in Figure 1.2, is much easier for a new user to understand and to use than the command-line prompt. (The DOS Shell for version numbers lower than DOS 6 looks a little different than the one shown here.)

Drive icons   Menu

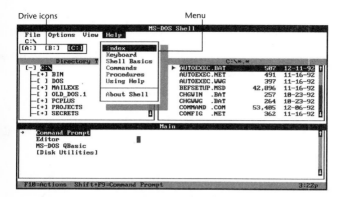

Figure 1.2 *Using the DOS Shell to issue commands is easier.*

In the DOS Shell, you give commands by selecting them from menus. A *menu* presents a list of choices for you to select from; with menus, you don't have to memorize command names in order to perform a DOS task. (You'll learn more about menus in Lesson 5.)

Some commands in the DOS Shell are issued by selecting a picture called an *icon*. (You'll learn more about the DOS Shell and using icons in Lessons 3 and 4.)

Come Out of Your Shell This book assumes that you are using the DOS Shell, because it is the easiest way to use DOS. The DOS Shell described in this book is the DOS 6 Shell, which is nearly identical to the DOS 5 Shell. (The DOS 4 Shell is substantially different.) If you prefer to enter commands at the DOS prompt, see the Command Reference at the end of this book.

Feel like you've been overwhelmed with DOS information? This is only the beginning! In the next lesson, you'll learn about disks, directories, and files.

Lesson 2

The Three D's: Disks, Directories, and de Files

Let's Start with Disks

As I mentioned earlier, there are two types of disks that your computer uses: *hard disks* and *floppy disks*. Hard disks are for permanent storage of files and programs. Floppy disks (often called *diskettes*) are for portable (removable) storage.

Under your computer's proverbial hood is a hard disk (usually referred to as drive C). It's used to store your programs, documents, and DOS. You can copy these files onto diskettes, where they serve as backups in case the hard disk gets damaged in some way.

Diskettes are small plastic squares with magnetic disks in them. Diskettes come in two sizes: 5 1/4-inches and 3 1/2-inches, as shown in Figure 2.1. Each size diskette comes in *high-density* and *double-density* versions. (3 1/2-inch diskettes also come in an *extended-density* version but we won't worry about that particular one because you probably won't be using it.)

Tip

Maybe I'm Dense, But Just What Does Disk Density Mean? Density refers to the amount of information a disk can hold. High-density diskettes hold at least twice as much information as the same size double-density diskettes because the information on high-density diskettes is packed closer together.

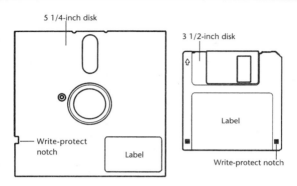

Figure 2.1   *Diskettes come in two sizes.*

The Destiny of Your Density!   Purchase diskettes that match the type of diskette drive your computer uses. This means you have to buy not only the right size diskette (5 1/4-inch or 3 1/2-inch), *but also the right density*. Make sure you know whether your computer has high-density disk drives. You can use double-density disks in high-density drives, but you can't use high-density disks at all if you don't have a high-density drive. (Yikes, this really is getting dense!)

To keep all this drive mumbo-jumbo straight, disk drives are assigned letters. Your computer's first diskette drive is called A, and a second drive is called B. Your computer's hard disk is called C, and any additional hard disks are called D, E, and so on. Disks are represented by their drive letter, followed by a colon, as in **C:** and **A:**.

What Are Files?

Hard disks and diskettes are used to store your *data*. (Computer geeks say "data" because it sounds more technical than "information," "grocery list," or "stuff.") You save your computer data in files, which are like the files you would keep in a filing cabinet. You store different kinds of data in different files. Each file has its own name.

A long time ago, the DOS masters decided that file names would have up to eight *characters* (letters or numbers) and a three digit *extension*, which helps to identify the contents or purpose of the file. For example, if you named a file GROSS.DOC, the extension .DOC would identify the file as a document file. Get it?

What Are Directories?

Because you can have thousands of files on your computer, you store them in directories so you know where they are. Directories help you stay organized. Directories are like trees. There's a root directory (usually drive C), then other directories branching out from it, and then subdirectories branching out from those directories. (Whoever thought that learning about computers would lead to forestry management?)

Let's examine our DOS tree. The root directory is represented by a single backslash (\), so the root directory of drive C is C:\. Only general-purpose files (such as the CONFIG.SYS and AUTOEXEC.BAT files, which DOS reads when booting) should be placed in the root directory.

Branching out from the root directory, you create other directories, one for each program you use. Try another analogy: a hallway. If you think of these directories as rooms, you could have a room for the Budget, Sales, Marketing, and so on, as shown in Figure 2.2.

You can separate the files you create (documents) from the program files (created by someone else) by creating subdirectories. To continue our room analogy, you could think of subdirectories as closets within each room. Directories are represented by a backslash, followed by the name of the directory, as in C:\SALES. Subdirectories are separated from their "room" by another backslash, as in C:\SALES\JOE.

Figure 2.2 *Organize your files in directories and subdirectories.*

In this lesson, you got bogged down with lots of details about disks, files, and directories. (I promise, it won't all be this mind-numbing.) Let's learn the reasons why working in the DOS Shell is much easier than working at the DOS prompt.

Lesson 3

The DOS Shell in a Nutshell

What's with All This DOS Shell Ballyhoo?

The DOS Shell is a *graphical interface*. A graphical interface uses pictures (called *icons*) to represent things such as drives and directories. The idea is that pictures are easier to understand than a bunch of confusing commands. If you ask me, pictures *are* easier to understand.

The Shell lets you perform common DOS commands more easily than you could with the DOS prompt. You start the DOS Shell manually by typing **DOSSHELL** and pressing **Enter**. You will then see a screen similar to Figure 3.1.

The DOS Shell has many parts:

Menu bar   Displays a list of pull-down menus.

Drive listing   Displays a list of drives.

Directory Tree   Displays a list of directories for the active drive.

File List   Displays a list of files in the active directory.

Program List   Displays a list of programs you can run, and program groups (collections of related programs).

Status bar   Displays a list of keys you can press to activate the menu bar or the DOS prompt.

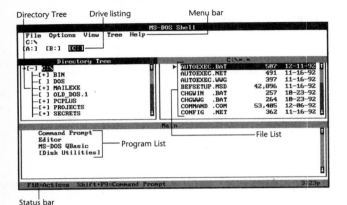

Status bar

Figure 3.1   The DOS Shell opening screen.

That's All Very Interesting, But How Do I Use It?

When you use the DOS Shell, I recommend performing most of the basic tasks with a mouse. The *mouse*, not related to the type found in cornfields, is a device attached to your computer which controls a pointer on your screen. To move the pointer to the left, move the mouse to the left. To move the pointer to the right, move the mouse to the right, and so on. To initiate most actions with the mouse, you either click or double-click; always use the left mouse button *unless told specifically to use the right*. Here are some common mouse actions:

Click   Press the mouse button once.

Double-click   Press the mouse button twice in rapid succession.

Drag To hold down the mouse button and move the mouse, all at the same time. (Don't chew gum while doing this or it will get really tricky!) First move the mouse to the starting position. Now hold down the mouse button. Drag the mouse to the ending position, and then release the mouse button.

To select a menu command with the mouse, click once on the menu name, and the menu freezes in the *drop-down*, or open, position. You can then move the mouse down the open menu list to the selection you want.

Get Me Back to the DOS Prompt!

If you are a diehard DOS command prompt person and you want to exit the DOS Shell and return to the DOS prompt, click on File in the menu bar to open the File menu, as shown in Figure 3.2. If you don't have a mouse, press **F10** to activate the menu bar, and then press **F**. Click on Exit, or press **X**.

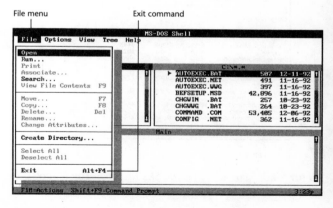

Figure 3.2   *Click on the File menu to open it.*

Quick Escape Okay, Houdini, to exit the DOS Shell quickly, press **F3**. This is like warp speed on a space ship.

Temporarily Out of Your Shell

You may want to leave the Shell temporarily to enter commands directly at the DOS command line. When you follow this procedure, the Shell is kept in memory, waiting until you come back to it.

To exit the DOS Shell temporarily, press **Shift+F9**, or click on **Command Prompt** in the **Program List**. The DOS prompt will be displayed, as shown in Figure 3.3. When you are ready to return to the DOS Shell, type **EXIT** at the prompt and press **Enter**.

Enter any DOS command you want.   DOS message

```
Microsoft(R) MS-DOS(R) Version 6
          (C)Copyright Microsoft Corp 1981-1993.

C:\>mem

Memory Type         Total =   Used   +   Free

Conventional         640K      196K      444K
Upper                155K       48K      107K
Adapter RAM/ROM      229K      229K        0K
Extended (XMS)      3072K     1396K     1676K
                    -----     -----     -----
Total memory        4096K     1868K     2228K

Total under 1 MB     795K      243K      552K

Largest executable program size       444K  (454800 bytes)
Largest free upper memory block       107K  (109904 bytes)
MS-DOS is resident in the high memory area.

C:\>EXIT
```

Type **EXIT** to return to Shell.

*Figure 3.3   You can exit the Shell temporarily by pressing
Shift+F9.*

A Quick Recap of the Exit Commands To leave the DOS Shell permanently, press **F3**. To leave the DOS Shell temporarily, press **Shift+F9**. To return to the DOS Shell after leaving it temporarily, type **EXIT**.

Now that you've learned how to play the DOS Shell game, you will learn how to move around the Shell window, and how to get help when you have absolutely no idea what you are doing.

Lesson 4

Shuffling Around in Your DOS Shell

Somehow, I Thought It Would Be Prettier Than This

Before you do anything else, try to change to *Graphics mode*. It is much nicer looking and has very cute little icons. When you started the DOS Shell, it was in *Text mode*, which can be used on all types of computer monitors. Text mode uses boxes and lines to represent the Shell icons, such as the disk drive and directory icons.

If your PC has a monitor that supports graphics, you'll probably want to change to Graphics mode, as shown in Figure 4.1. (For a comparison, look back at Figure 3.1, which depicts the Shell in Text mode. Eeeww!)

To change the DOS Shell to Graphics mode, open the Options menu by clicking on it. If you do not have a mouse, press F10 to activate the menu bar, and then press O. Select the Display command by clicking on it. If you are using the keyboard, press D. A dialog box, shown in Figure 4.2, will appear (you'll learn more about dialog boxes in the next lesson).

Click on the desired graphics resolution, or use the arrow keys to highlight a Graphics selection, press **Enter**, and . . . Shazam! Your screen will change to Graphics mode.

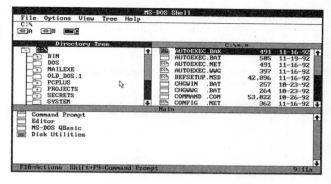

Figure 4.1 *The DOS Shell in Graphics mode.*

Figure 4.2 *The Display dialog box.*

> **Reading the Fine Print** The higher the *resolution*, the greater the number of lines that will display, but the letters appear tinier. So, if you select a high resolution (such as Graphics 43 Lines), more files and directories will appear on-screen, but the letters will be smaller and harder to read. Make sure you feel comfortable with the resolution you select.

Moving Around the Shell Window

The DOS Shell window is made up of several sections (see Figure 4.3): the drive listing, the Directory Tree, the File List, and the Program List. The *active* section is always the one that's highlighted.

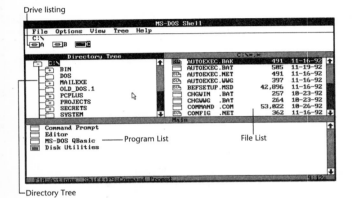

Figure 4.3 *The DOS Shell window is divided into sections.*

To move from section to section with the mouse, you simply click inside that section. To move from section to section with the keyboard, press the **Tab** key. To move backward from section to section, press **Shift+Tab**. Pretty easy so far, isn't it?

How Do I Change Drives?

Say you want to see the files on the disk in drive A instead of the ones on the hard disk. You can change the display so it reflects the contents of drive A.

To select drive A in the Drive listing, press **Tab** to activate the Drive listing section. (The title bar will be highlighted, which means it will be in a different color than the other title bars.) Use the arrow keys to highlight drive A and press **Enter**.

If you use a mouse, you can simply click on the **drive** A icon. The Directory Tree and the File List will change to reflect the contents of drive A. To change drives in one step, press **Ctrl+*drive***. For example, to change to drive A, press **Ctrl+A**.

Command Line Users This is an easy one. To change drives at the DOS command line, enter the drive letter followed by a colon, as in **A:** or **C:**.

Help Wanted!

Getting help within the DOS Shell is a piece of cake. Any time you need help, remember the magic help key: **F1**. The Help feature is *context-sensitive*, which means it'll give you help for whatever it thinks you are trying to do. For example, if the Program List is active, and the selection Command Prompt is highlighted, when you press **F1**, you will see a screen like the one shown in Figure 4.4.

```
┌─────────────────────── MS-DOS Shell Help ───────────────────────┐
│          ████████████ Help For Command Prompt ████████████        │
│ Starts the MS-DOS command prompt where you can type any MS-DOS  ↑ │
│ command.                                                          │
│                                                                   │
│ To return to MS-DOS Shell from the command line:                  │
│                                                                   │
│ 1. Type exit                                                      │
│ 2. Press ENTER.                                                   │
│                                                                   │
│ Related Topic                                                     │
│ ▓More on Command Prompt▓ ─────────────────── Jump topic           │
│                        ☾   ─·─                                    │
│                                                                 ↓ │
├───────────────────────────────────────────────────────────────────┤
│  ( Close )   ( Back )   ( Keys )   ( Index )   ( Help )           │
└───────────────────────────────────────────────────────────────────┘
```

Figure 4.4   Getting help in the DOS Shell is easy.

Tell Me More   Some Help topics contain more information than can be displayed on a single screen. To see more, press the **Page Down** key.

Some Help windows provide a quick means of getting additional information, called *jump topics*. For example, if you wanted more information on the DOS command prompt, you would select the related jump topic, **More on Command Prompt**. To jump to a topic, press **Tab** until the topic is highlighted, and press **Enter**. Or you can double-click on the desired topic.

Command Line Users   Need some help? To get Help with a DOS command, type that command, followed by **/?**. For example, to get Help for the MEM command, type **MEM /?** or **HELP MEM**.

To exit Help, press **Esc**.

In this lesson, you learned how to do some basic gallivanting around in the DOS Shell. You are now ready to learn how to use the famous menus and dialog boxes that are so much quicker than using the command prompt.

Lesson 5

Ordering from the Menu: Using Menus and Dialog Boxes

Menu Basics

Pull-down menus are the best things about the DOS Shell. In fact, they're about the best things since peanut butter and microwave ovens. They're called pull-down menus because they work like a window shade; you pull them down to use them. You use them to choose commands, instead of typing in commands like you do at the DOS prompt. See the menu bar at the top of the DOS Shell window shown in Figure 5.1? It lists the main DOS Shell menus: File, Options, View, Tree, and Help. You can find all sorts of commands under each of these menus.

You can tell a lot about a command by the way it looks on the menu (who said looks aren't important?):

Grayed text Commands that are currently unavailable will be grayed, or shaded out, which means you can't select them.

Shortcut keys A single letter of a menu command, such as **x** in Exit, that can be used to activate the command with the keyboard. Shortcut keys appear as underlined letters on the main menu. In this book, shortcut keys appear as bold letters, as in File.

Accelerator keys Like shortcut keys, these can be used to activate the command with the keyboard. Usually a function key (or a key combination, such as Alt+F4), these are displayed next to the menu command.

Ellipsis An ellipsis is that three dot thing that appears after some menu commands, such as the File Search... command. An ellipsis tells you that a dialog box will appear if you choose the command, which means you'll have to provide more specific information.

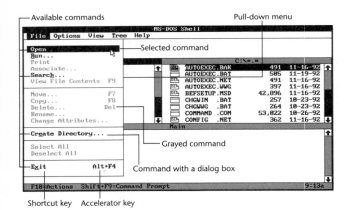

Figure 5.1   The delightful DOS Shell's menu system.

How Do I Select the Menu Commands?

To activate a pull-down menu with the mouse, click once on the menu name. To activate a pull-down menu with the keyboard, you can do one of two things:

☞ Press **Alt** plus the shortcut key. For example, to activate the File pull-down menu, press **Alt+F**.

or,

☞ Press **F10**, and then use the arrow keys to activate the appropriate pull-down menu.

Once a menu is visible, you can select a command from it by clicking on the command or by using one of two different keyboard methods:

☞ Use the arrow keys to highlight the command, and then press **Enter**.

or,

☞ Press the shortcut key letter for the command. For example, with the File menu open, you can select the Search... command by pressing the letter **H**.

What Should I Do When a Dialog Box Appears?

No need to panic when a dialog box appears, DOS just wants to force more information out of you. Dialog boxes very rarely ask for any mind-boggling information. A typical dialog box is shown in Figure 5.2.

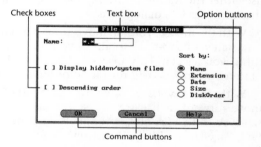

Figure 5.2   A typical dialog box.

There are a few optional components of dialog boxes that you should familiarize yourself with:

List box   Presents a list of items to choose from, such as a list of files.

Text box   Lets you type or edit information, such as the name of a file.

Drop-down list box   Displays under the main list item, like a window shade. Drop-down list boxes are like normal list boxes, except that the list does not display until activated.

Check box   Indicates options that can be turned on or off, such as Read Only.

Option button   Selects mutually exclusive options, such as sorting files by name or extension.

Command button   Performs some specific command, such as OK or Cancel.

How Do I Select the Stuff I Want?

Some dialog boxes will have many different components, but usually, they only have a couple. You can use either the mouse or the keyboard when making these choices in a dialog box.

With the mouse, you can move around by clicking on whatever you want. Usually, if you click on something, you select it. This means that if you click on an option button, you will turn it on or off, or *toggle* it.

With the keyboard, press **Tab** or **Shift+Tab** to move forward or backward. Use the arrow keys to select stuff. In a list box, you can also use the Home, End, Page Up, and Page Down keys. You can use the Spacebar to toggle options on or off.

Here are some standard command buttons you can select in dialog boxes:

OK   Select this button to execute the choices you made and close the dialog box.

Cancel   Select this button if you change your mind and want to cancel your choices and return to the DOS Shell.

Help   Select this button when you're in a jam.

You now have a few tricks up your DOS sleeve about using menus and dialog boxes. In the next lesson, you will learn how to exert all kinds of control over the DOS Shell window, which is really great for domineering personality types.

Lesson 6

I'll Do It My Way: Controlling the Shell Window

I'd Like to Change Directories, I Think

You can pretty much make the Shell do whatever you want. If the Shell window displays the contents of the current drive and that's not the one you want to look at, change it.

Activate the Directory Tree (use the skills you learned in the previous lessons to move around the screen). Change directories by clicking on a new directory or by using the arrow keys to highlight it. The File List will change to display the contents of the new directory.

The Root of All DOS Evil   To move quickly to the root directory, press the backslash key (\).

Command Line Users   Meanwhile, back at the DOS prompt, the equivalent DOS command for changing directories is CHDIR or plain old CD.

Now I'd Like to Change the Way This Directory Is Displayed

Say you've got gobs of subdirectories cluttering up the place. If there's a minus sign in the folder next to the directory, that means all its subdirectories are displayed. If you don't want them to be displayed, click on the minus sign. It'll change to a plus and your subdirectories will be hidden. Brilliant!

This minus and plus business is called *collapsing* and *expanding* your directory tree. You also can use the Tree menu to do this if you want.

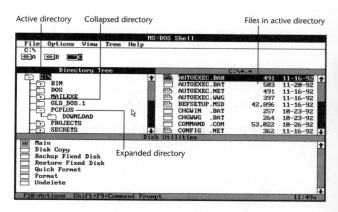

Figure 6.1   *The DOS Shell window reflects the contents of the current drive.*

Expanding a Directory Branch

To expand a directory branch, select the directory to expand. Then, click on the + (in front of the directory name), or press plus (+). When you expand a directory branch, it expands one level. If there are sub-directories, they won't be displayed. Press the asterisk (*) to expand a directory through all of its levels.

Fast Expansion To expand all branches of the Directory Tree, press **Ctrl+asterisk (*)**. Careful, it will make your head spin, it goes so fast!

Collapsing a Directory Branch

To collapse a directory branch, first select the branch of the directory you want to collapse. Then click on the minus sign (–) in front of the directory name, or press minus (–). If you have expanded the entire Directory Tree and want to display only the directories off the root, press **backslash (\)** to move to the root directory, press minus (–) to collapse all directories, and then press plus (+) to expand one level.

I Think I'll Change My Files Now

You can change the way files are displayed in the File List with the Options File Display Options command. Select from among these options:

- ☞ **Name**   Use this option to select which files are displayed.
- ☞ **Display hidden/system files**   Some files (especially the operating system files) are hidden from you for your own good. You can display these files with this option.
- ☞ **Sort by**   Use this option to change the way files are sorted in the File List.
- ☞ **Descending order**   Use this option to sort files in reverse order.

To change the way file information is displayed, first, open the Options menu, and then select the File Display Options command. The File Display Options dialog box will appear, as shown in Figure 6.2. Select the desired options, and click on **OK**, or press **Enter**.

Figure 6.2 *The File Display Options dialog box.*

Command Line Users The DOS command for displaying the files in a directory and controlling the order in which they are displayed is the DIR command.

I Need More Than One File List

Some DOS functions, such as copying files or moving them from one directory to another, are easier with a dual list display, as shown in Figure 6.3.

You use the View menu to display dual file lists. Select the **D**ual File Lists command. Two file lists will appear. If you want to return to a single file list, you can choose that option from the View menu also. You can also choose a thing called Program/File Lists, which shows both a single file list and the Program List.

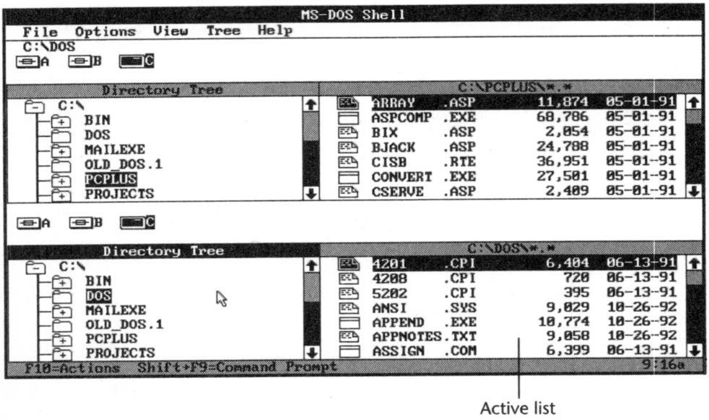

Active list

Figure 6.3 *Using dual file lists can make some DOS functions easier.*

Now that you've shown DOS who's boss when you controlled the information displayed in the Directory Tree and File List windows, you are ready to select files, which is a very important thing to learn.

Lesson 7

Selecting Files in the DOS Shell

Eeny, Meeny, Miny, Mo

You can't really do anything with your files until you tell DOS which files you want to work with. Actually, it's one of the few things about DOS that makes perfect sense to me. How is DOS supposed to know which files you want to copy, remove, or rename unless you specify them? DOS is no genius, and certainly isn't a mind reader. (Disappointing to learn, huh?)

When a file is *selected*, it appears highlighted on your screen. To select a single file, either click on it or use the arrow keys to highlight it. If you want to select all the files in the current directory, press **Ctrl+/** (slash).

Make sure you only click once on the file to select it. If you double-click, you will open the file. If it's a program file, you'll run the program. Yikes!

Selecting multiple files (but not all the files) is a little bit trickier. We'll start out with files that are next to each other in the File List, since that's easier. (By the way, files that are in order are called *contiguous*.) To select these files, click on the first file you want, then hold down the **Shift** key, and click on the last file you want. Your files will all show up highlighted, like in Figure 7.1.

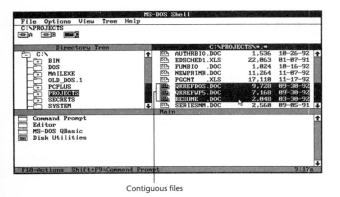

Contiguous files

Figure 7.1 *Here are some selected contiguous files.*

You can select contiguous files with the keyboard by using the arrow keys to move to the first file, then holding down the **Shift** key and using the arrow keys to move to the last file. The files will become selected as you go along.

My Files Are Out of Order

Let's say you want to select a file here, a file there, and maybe a file so far away that you have to use the Page Down key to get to it. These are called *noncontiguous* files because, you guessed it, they aren't next to each other.

Selecting them is easy with the mouse. You just hold down the **Ctrl** key, and click on whichever files you want. If you accidentally click on one you don't want, you can click on it again (while still holding down **Ctrl**) to deselect it.

It's a little more involved when you use the keyboard. You have to first move to the file you want using the arrow keys. Then, press **Shift+F8**. You'll see the word **Add** appear in the status bar, as shown in

Figure 7.2. Use the arrow keys to move to the files you want to select, toggling the highlighting on and off with the **Spacebar**. When you're done, press **Shift+F8** again so you won't be in Add mode anymore.

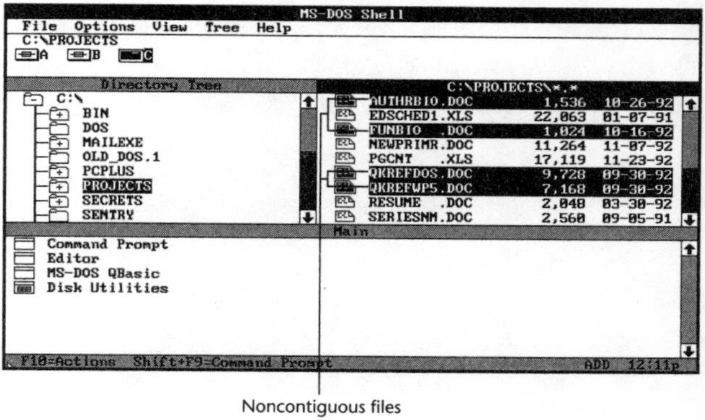

Noncontiguous files

Figure 7.2 *Selecting noncontiguous files isn't as much of a hassle as you might think.*

But the Files I Want Aren't in the Same File List

Uh-oh, now you've done it. You are really asking for a lot from DOS, you know, by wanting to select files in different directories. Not to worry, DOS grudgingly lets you select all the files you want from any directory with the Select Across Directories command.

You can turn on the Select Across Directories option from the Options menu. When you turn it on, you can move to other directories and go around selecting all the files you want. Whenever you want to turn the option off, just select it from the Options menu again.

Although you may not realize it, I was secretly preparing you for the next lesson by showing you how to select files in this lesson. (I'm such a little trickster.) Now you can learn how to copy your selected files. Doesn't that sound like a hoot?

Lesson 8

Cloning 101: Copying Files

A Word to the Wise

If you've jumped ahead to this lesson without reading Lesson 7, you might want to skip back and review the steps for selecting files. Also, if you start selecting files and you notice that files from other directories are being selected (and you don't want them to be), you left the Select Across Directories option on.

Command Line Users Okay die-hard DOS prompt people, the equivalent DOS command for copying files is COPY. Big surprise, eh?

Playing CopyCat with the Mouse

When you copy files, the original file is left alone, and a copy is placed in the directory you indicate. If you are copying to a different directory, it's easier if you choose the Dual File Lists display from the View menu so you can see what's going on.

To copy files, first select the files to copy. Then, while holding down the **Ctrl** key, drag the files to the directory in the Directory Tree (*not* the File List) where you want them copied. The Ghostbuster-type No symbol (a circle with a diagonal slash through it) will appear, but as you move the icon to a valid directory on the screen, it will change to look like little files, as shown in Figure 8.1.

When you release the mouse button, a confirmation box will appear, asking if you really want to copy the files. Click on **Yes**.

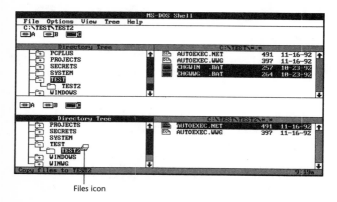

Files icon

Figure 8.1 *Copying files with the mouse.*

I Thought You Looked Familiar . . . If you attempt to copy a file into a directory where a file of the same name already exists, DOS will ask if you want to replace (overwrite) the original file with the one you are copying.

Copying Files with the (Yawn) Keyboard

Copying files with the keyboard is not as easy as with a mouse, but I know some of you are just dying to know how to do it, so I'll tell you. First, select the files to copy. Then, you open the File menu, and select the Copy command. The Copy File dialog box will appear, as shown in Figure 8.2.

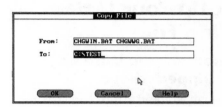

Figure 8.2   The Copy File dialog box.

The selected files will appear in the From box. Type the destination directory in the To box. For example, to copy files to a directory called STINKY on drive C, type **C:\STINKY**. To copy files to a subdirectory called YUCKY, which is under a directory called STINKY on drive C, type **C:\STINKY\YUCKY**. To copy files to the default directory on another drive, type the drive letter, as in **A:**.

Press **Enter** when you're finished fooling around, and the files are copied.

Instant Copy   To copy files quickly, select them, and press **F8**. It's another warp speed trick.

In this lesson, you learned how to copy files like a pro. Want to learn how to move things around? Let's go.

Lesson 9

Pack Up Your U-Haul, We're Moving Files

For Those of You Wise Guys Who Skipped Ahead

If you jumped ahead to this chapter, I suggest that you turn back to Lesson 7 and review how to select files. You'll need to know how to select stuff before you can move it. Also, if you find that all sorts of files are being selected in other directories (and you don't want them to be) turn off the Select Across Directories command from the Options menu.

Command Line Users DOS 6 has a command for moving files: MOVE. Unfortunately, earlier versions don't have the command, so in that case, you have to copy files to a new location, and then delete the old ones. (Another good reason why you should upgrade to DOS 6, if you haven't already.)

Moving Files with the Mouse

When you move files, the original is deleted and a copy is placed in the selected directory. Moving files with the mouse is strikingly similar to copying them. You select the files, and then hold down the **Alt** key while you drag the files to the new directory in the Directory Tree (*not* the File List).

That pesky ghostbuster-like No symbol will appear, but as soon as you move the files to a valid directory, the symbol will change to look like little files. When you release the mouse button, a confirmation box will appear asking if you really want to move the files. Click on **Yes**.

Moving Files with the Keyboard

Moving files with the keyboard is, again, similar to copying files with the keyboard. After you select the files to copy, open the File menu, and select the **Move** command. The Move File dialog box will appear, as shown in Figure 9.1.

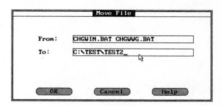

Figure 9.1 The Move File dialog box.

The selected files will appear in the From box. Type the destination directory in the To box. For example, to move files to a directory called OINK on drive C, type **C:\OINK**. To move files to a subdirectory called PIGLET that is under a directory called OINK on drive C, type **C:\OINK\PIGLET**. To move files to the default directory on another drive, type the drive letter, as in A:.

Press **Enter** when you're done with the dialog box, and the files are moved.

Quick Moves   To move files quickly, select them and press **F7**. Hold onto your seat; it's a quick trip.

Now that you've learned how to move stuff, you can truck on over to the next lesson where you'll learn how to rename things.

Lesson 10

What's In a Name?

Rules and Regulations for Renaming

DOS will let you rename files, but you have to obey certain rules. These are the same rules you had to follow when you named the file in the first place, so remembering them should be no sweat. Here they are:

- ☛ File names may contain up to eight characters plus an optional three character extension.

- ☛ Don't use any of these characters:
  space . / \ [ ] : * | + ; , ?

- ☛ Use a period only to separate the file name from the extension, as in NONSENSE.DOC. (You cannot include a period as part of the file name.)

You have to follow the same rules when naming directories, although most users do not use an extension when naming a directory. For example, you could name a directory HOOEY.93 instead of just HOOEY, but that would be confusing (the directory could easily be mistaken for a file.)

Command Line Users The equivalent DOS command for renaming files is REN. To rename a directory, use the MOVE command (if you're using DOS 6).

So How Do I Rename This Puppy?

To rename a file or directory, first select the file or directory to rename. Open the File menu, and select the Rename command. The Rename File or Rename Directory dialog box will appear, as shown in Figure 10.1.

Enter the new name for the file or directory in the New name text box. Type the complete name, including the extension. Press **Enter**, or click on **OK**, and the file or directory is renamed.

Figure 10.1 *The Rename File dialog box is similar to the Rename Directory dialog box.*

Everyone's Changing Their Names   You can rename more than one file or directory at a time by selecting them *before* using the File Rename command. A different dialog box will appear for each file or directory you selected.

As you've learned, renaming files and directories can be a handy thing to know how to do. In the next lesson, you will learn how to delete files and how to get them back when you didn't mean to delete them.

Lesson 11

Spring Cleaning: Deleting Files (and Getting Them Back)

To Delete or Not to Delete

You will find yourself deleting files for many reasons: the files are outdated and you no longer use them, you accidentally saved the same file 38 times, or you need to make room on your hard drive. Make absolutely sure that you don't need the file any more before you delete it. If your boss asks for a report that you deleted two weeks ago, you'll be in big trouble.

This Darn Hard Drive Is All Congested (Take two disks and call me in the morning.) If you have too many files on your hard drive, copy some of the files onto floppy diskettes and delete them from your hard drive. That way, you still have them around if you need them later.

To delete files, first select the files to delete. Then, press the **Del** key. If you've selected more than one file, the Delete File dialog box will appear as shown in Figure 11.1.

Select **OK**, and the Delete Files Confirmation dialog box is displayed for each file selected. Select **Yes** to confirm the deletion of each file. To bypass a file (not delete it), select **No**. If at any time during the deletion process you change your mind, press **Esc** to cancel.

Figure 11.1   *When you delete more than one file, a list of files is displayed.*

Command Line Users   Attention prompt maniacs, the equivalent DOS command for deleting files is DEL.

Uh-Oh, I Accidentally Deleted the Wrong File

First of all, don't panic if you delete a file by mistake. However, *don't do anything* until you try to get it back. If you've done something crazy like save or copy documents since you deleted the file, you might not be able to undelete it (now you can panic).

See, DOS doesn't really delete files when you tell it to. It erases the file's *record*: the file's name and location. But unless new data has overwritten the deleted file, it's still there. Still confused? This is how it actually works: when DOS erases the file's name from its records, it merely changes the first letter of its name to a question mark, as in ?ONSENSE.DOC. DOS knows not to pay attention to any file that begins with a question mark, so the space that the file occupies becomes available. If another file needs the disk space, it is written over the deleted file, replacing the old data.

To undelete a file, change to the directory that contained the deleted file. From the Program List in

the View menu, select **Disk Utilities**, then select
Undelete. The Undelete dialog box, shown in Figure
11.2, appears.

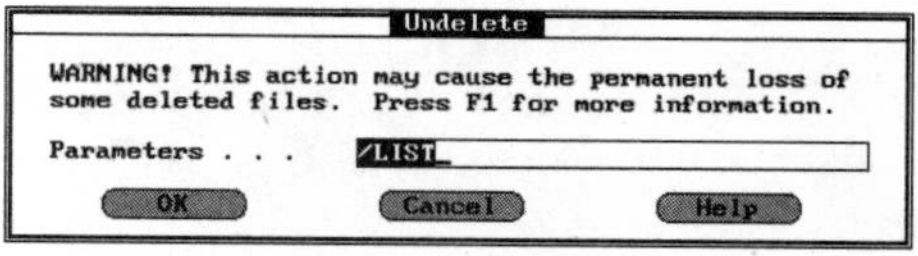

Figure 11.2   *The Undelete dialog box.*

If you know the name of the deleted file, type its
name in the Parameters text box. Otherwise, type ***.***
to list all the recently deleted files in this directory,
and press **Enter**. A listing of files will appear, as shown
in Figure 11.3. Press Y to confirm the undelete procedure. If you don't want to undelete a particular file,
press N. You might have a whole slew of files if you've
just done a lot of deleting. To stop the list and return
to the Shell, press **Esc**.

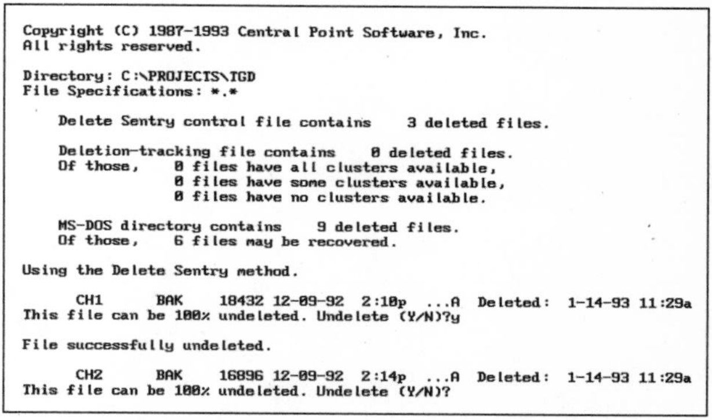

```
Copyright (C) 1987-1993 Central Point Software, Inc.
All rights reserved.

Directory: C:\PROJECTS\TGD
File Specifications: *.*

    Delete Sentry control file contains    3 deleted files.

    Deletion-tracking file contains    0 deleted files.
    Of those,    0 files have all clusters available,
                 0 files have some clusters available,
                 0 files have no clusters available.

    MS-DOS directory contains    9 deleted files.
    Of those,    6 files may be recovered.

Using the Delete Sentry method.

    CH1      BAK    18432 12-09-92  2:18p  ...A  Deleted:  1-14-93 11:29a
This file can be 100% undeleted. Undelete (Y/N)?y

File successfully undeleted.

    CH2      BAK    16896 12-09-92  2:14p  ...A  Deleted:  1-14-93 11:29a
This file can be 100% undeleted. Undelete (Y/N)?
```

Figure 11.3   *Undelete lists recently deleted files.*

If you're asked, politely enter the first letter of the deleted file. DOS will display a message telling you whether you were successful or not.

Do You See What I See?   If your recovered file is not immediately listed in the File List, press **F5** to refresh the File List window.

Yo! Command Line Users   The equivalent DOS command for recovering deleted files is UNDELETE.

In this lesson, you learned how to destroy files and how to get them back when you didn't mean to destroy them (oops). Now it's time to learn how to format diskettes with the best of them. Follow me!

Lesson 12

Somebody's Gotta Do It: Formatting Disks

Do I *Have* to Format My Disks?

You don't have to format your disks. You can shell out the extra clams and buy them pre-formatted in the store, but you really shouldn't. Not only are you wasting your money paying someone else to do a simple task that you can do yourself in very little time, but disks that are formatted in the drive in which you'll be using them are generally more reliable.

When you format diskettes, all you're doing is preparing them for use and erasing all information that might be on them. However, you have to follow more DOS rules (ugh!) when formatting.

First of all, diskettes must be formatted to the proper *density*. In Lesson 2, you learned that the density of a diskette determines the amount of information it can hold. If you use diskettes that match the density of your computer's diskette drives, you won't have to worry about formatting them incorrectly. By default, diskettes are formatted to the density of the drive they occupy.

To format a disk, first place the diskette in the disk drive. Open the **Disk Utilities** menu in the **Program List**, and then select the **Format** command. The Format dialog box appears, shown in Figure 12.1.

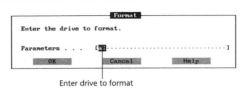

Enter drive to format

Figure 12.1 *The Format dialog box.*

If it's necessary, type the drive letter to format, followed by a colon (for example, **A:**) in the Parameters text box. Select **OK**, and you will be prompted to insert the diskette. Press **Enter**, and DOS formats the diskette.

After the disk is formatted, you can type an optional volume label, up to 11 characters (including spaces). The volume label is the name you can give each of your disks so you know what they contain. For example, if the disk will contain miscellaneous ramblings, you could name it BUNK. Press **Enter** when you are through.

To format another diskette of the same density, type **Y** at the **Format another (Y/N)?** prompt, and press **Enter**. When you are through, press **Enter** to return to the DOS Shell.

After a diskette is formatted, DOS displays the amount of space available on the diskette, as shown in Figure 12.2.

Attention Command Line Users! The equivalent DOS command for formatting diskettes is FORMAT.

Make It Quick If the diskette has already been formatted, and you simply want to erase the files, use the Quick Format command on the Disk Utilities menu.

```
Insert new diskette for drive A:
and press ENTER when ready...

Checking existing disk format.
Saving UNFORMAT information.
Verifying 1.2M
Format complete.

Volume label (11 characters, ENTER for none)? jan budget

   1213952 bytes total disk space
   1213952 bytes available on disk

       512 bytes in each allocation unit.
      2371 allocation units available on disk.

Volume Serial Number is 183A-16E9

Format another (Y/N)?
```

Enter Y to format another diskette   Amount of available disk space

Figure 12.2 DOS displays the amount of space on the formatted diskette.

For a Change of Pace . . .

You can make a *bootable diskette* to boot your system in the case of an emergency. It's a good idea to have one on hand, so you should make one now while you're thinking about it. All you have to do is format the disk like usual until you get to that part where you have to enter the drive letter to format. Type the drive letter to format, then add the /S switch, like this: **A: / S**. Then just complete the rest of the formatting steps like usual.

Tip

Why Do I Use the /S Switch? The /S switch tells DOS to copy the system files onto the diskette, making it bootable.

Another variation outside the norm of formatting is when you have to format a double-density diskette in a high-density drive. In this situation, you would complete the usual steps for formatting a diskette until you get to the part where you enter the drive letter. After you type in the drive letter, use the /F: switch followed by the size of the diskette in bytes, like this: **A: /F:360**. Then complete the rest of the formatting steps like normal.

Uh-Oh, I Don't Think I Should Have Formatted That Disk

You might be able to unformat a diskette that you or some lunkhead formatted accidentally. (The creators of DOS just *knew* this was going to happen.) To unformat a diskette, first place the diskette in its drive, then exit the DOS Shell temporarily by pressing **Shift+F9**.

Type **UNFORMAT** *drive*: where *drive:* is replaced by the letter of the diskette drive, as in UNFORMAT A:. When prompted, type **Y** to proceed with the unformat. When the unformat is completed, you can return to the DOS Shell. To return, type **EXIT** at the prompt.

In this lesson, you learned how to format and unformat diskettes. Next, you will learn how to control your directories when they get all obnoxious and unruly. Step this way!

Lesson 13

Delinquent Directories (Controlling Directories When They Get Out of Hand)

I Have Too Many Files; I Need Another Directory

You can add directories to organize your files and make your life easier. For example, if you use a word processor, you could add a subdirectory (under your word processing directory) called MYSTUFF or WORK to store the documents you create. If more than one person uses your computer, it's a good idea to create directories where each person can store their files.

Before you create a directory, decide whether it will be a subdirectory of an existing directory. If so, select the parent directory in the Directory Tree. (If no directory is selected, the new directory will be a subdirectory of the root.)

Open the File menu, and select the Create Directory command. The Create Directory dialog box, shown in Figure 13.1, appears. Type the name of the new directory to create (up to eight characters). Select OK, and the directory will be created.

Command Line Users Meanwhile, back at the old DOS prompt, the equivalent DOS command for creating directories is MD or MKDIR (an abbreviation of make directory).

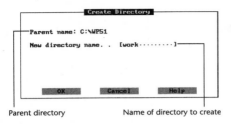

Parent directory   Name of directory to create

Figure 13.1   The Create Directory dialog box.

I Have Too Many Directories; I Need to Delete Some

Sometimes, this whole business of creating directories and subdirectories can get way out of hand. Soon, you'll have directories hanging around all over and getting generally unruly if you aren't careful. You should delete the directories that you no longer use.

You cannot delete a directory which contains files or subdirectories. You must delete those things first. However, there is a very cool DOS prompt command (DELTREE) that you can use instead of the procedure described here. The DELTREE command will delete a directory *and* all of its subdirectories and files. Amazing!

To delete a directory in the DOS Shell, select the directory to delete. If necessary, delete all files and subdirectories. Press **Del**, and then select **Yes**. Relatively painless, wasn't it?

So Long, Farewell, auf Wiedersehen, Good-bye   If you delete the directory in which files were stored, you may not be able to undelete the files.

Command Line Users   The equivalent DOS command for deleting directories is RD (remove directory). To delete an entire directory tree, including subdirectories and files, use the DELTREE command.

Now that you know how to make your directories manageable, let's discuss backing up your hard disk and why it's so important.

Lesson 14

Backup: A Computer Plumbing Problem or a Precaution?

An Overview of Backup

A *backup* is a copy of the files on your hard disk. It is very important that you make backups of your system so that if anything ever happens to it, you won't lose everything. Backups can take a long time and a lot of disks, depending on how much you have on your computer. For example, I have so much stuff on my computer that it takes 132 floppy disks to store it all on. (Unfortunately, I'm not joking.) Keep that in mind.

There are three types of backups:

Full backup   This backup makes a complete copy of every file on your hard disk.

Incremental backup   This backup copies only the files that have been changed since the last full or incremental backup. To restore a complete hard disk, you would need *your full backup and all incremental backup diskettes*.

Differential backup   This backup copies only the files that have been changed since the last full backup. A differential backup may take longer than an incremental backup. To restore a complete hard disk, *you would need your full backup and latest differential backup diskettes*.

Now Here's a Plan As a rule of thumb, perform a full backup once a month, then perform either an incremental or differential backup at the end of each work day. If you don't perform your full backups often, then use an incremental backup every day, because it won't take as long as a differential backup.

To perform a backup, you must select the drives, directories, and the files to be backed up. These selections can be stored permanently in a *setup file*. MS Backup comes with a few setup files already created for common situations, such as a full backup.

The first time you run MS Backup, it will *configure* itself. To do this, MS Backup will run some tests on your system. You will need two diskettes of the same size and density as the diskettes you will use when you do real backups. Follow the on-screen instructions, and remember to save the configuration when the tests are over.

I Want It All: Performing a Full Backup

To perform a full backup, open the **Disk Utilities** menu in the **Program List**. If the Program List is not displayed on your screen, select Program/File Lists from the View menu. Select **MS Backup**, and then choose Backup. The Backup dialog box, shown in Figure 14.1, appears.

In the Backup From box, select the drive to back up. MS Backup will display **All Files** next to the drive letter you select. If you are going to use diskettes of a different type or size from the one listed, change the drive letter in the Backup To box. Select Start Backup. When the backup is complete, press **Enter** to return to the Shell.

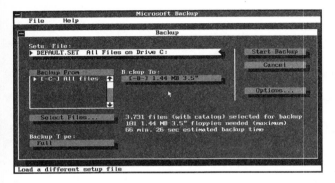

Figure 14.1 *You can configure your backup from the Backup dialog box.*

Command Line Users From the DOS prompt, use the command MSBACKUP to start the MS Backup program, and back up your hard drive as described in this lesson.

I Don't Want To Do a Full Backup If you want to do an incremental or differential backup, select the appropriate one in the Backup Type box.

I Only Want to Back Up Certain Files You can select the files you want to back up. Go through all the steps described earlier, and after you specify the drive in the Backup From box, choose Select Files. A dialog box will appear that lets you choose the ones you want. An arrow indicates the files and directories that have been toggled on or off. When you're done selecting, choose **OK**.

In this lesson, you learned how to back up your hard disk. Now you can read about restoring files to your hard disk, if for some reason your hard disk doesn't want to use the old files any more.

Lesson 15

Yikes! My Hard Disk Is Ruined! (How Do I Restore It?)

Restoring a Full Backup When There's No Other Way

Sometimes, your computer might unexplainably go on the fritz. Or you might accidentally format your hard drive. (This is, in case you hadn't guessed, an extremely bad and excrutiatingly embarrassing thing to do. I knew a guy who formatted his hard drive once. He's never lived it down.) If your computer completely crashes and there's nothing you can do, you'll have to restore your files from the backup disks you conscientiously prepared. To restore a full backup, open the **Disk Utilities** menu in the Program List. Select **MS Backup**, then choose **Restore**. The Restore dialog box, shown in Figure 15.1, appears.

In the Restore Files box, select the drive to restore. Use the drive that the files were backed up from, regardless of whether you want to restore the files to a different drive. **All Files** will display next to the drive letter you select. If you are going to use diskettes of a different type or size from the one listed, change the drive letter in the Restore From box. If you want to restore files to different drives or directories from which they were backed up, select **Restore To**. Select **Start Restore**. When the restore is complete, press **Enter** to return to the Shell.

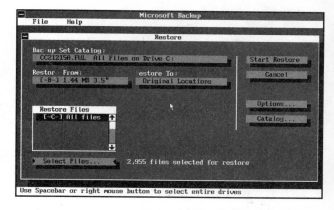

Figure 15.1 *You can configure your restoration from the Restore dialog box.*

Command Line Users At the DOS prompt, use the command MSBACKUP to start the MS Backup program and restore files to your hard drive as described in this lesson.

I Don't Want to Restore the Whole Thing

You may want to restore only certain directories or files. By restoring only the files or directories you need, you can reduce the time it takes to do a full restore.

To restore selected directories or files, run through the steps as usual, but after you select the drive whose files you want to restore, choose Select Files. The Select Restore Files dialog box appears. Select the directories or files you want to restore. Selected directories have an arrow beside them, selected files have check marks.

If more than one version of a file exists on your different backup sets, the most recent version is the one DOS restores. You can select a different version by using Version from the Select Restore Files dialog box.

Using Special in the Select Restore Files dialog box, you can exclude additional files from restoration, such as system and hidden files.

In this lesson, you learned how to restore files if they become damaged. Look at the next page to start learning how to keep your system safe from those nasty things called viruses. Aachoo!

Lesson 16

Virus Got You Down?

What Is a Computer Virus and Do I Need a Doctor?

A *virus* is a program that infects your computer in various ways, such as changing your files, damaging your disks, and preventing your computer from starting. Bad news, indeed!

You can infect your system any time you copy or download files onto your disk, or boot from a diskette. You can protect yourself from serious damage by:

- ☞ Maintaining a recent backup of your files.

- ☞ Checking diskettes for viruses before copying files from them. *Be sure to check program disks before installing new software.*

- ☞ Write-protecting program diskettes to prevent infection.

- ☞ Running VSafe, a special DOS 6 virus-detection program, all the time.

- ☞ Taking your computer to the vet for its rabies shots. Oh no, wait, that's the dog. Okay, skip this one.

- ☞ Never starting your computer with a diskette in the drive. (Make a virus-free bootable diskette for emergency purposes; see the next section.)

- ☞ Running Microsoft Anti-Virus (another DOS 6 program) as soon as a problem occurs.

Creating a Startup Diskette

You can create a virus-safe startup diskette by following the instructions in Lesson 12. After the diskette is formatted, add the CONFIG.SYS, AUTOEXEC.BAT, MSAV.EXE, and MSAV.HLP files to it.

Safety Precaution Keep your system files current by copying your CONFIG.SYS and AUTOEXEC.BAT files onto your emergency-startup diskette whenever you modify them. What are CONFIG.SYS and AUTOEXEC.BAT, you ask? Turn to Lesson 18 to find out.

After you've copied these files onto the diskette, write-protect it to prevent infection. This means putting a sticky tab over the square hole near the top of a 5.25-inch disk or pushing the tab up on the back of a 3.5-inch disk. When you write-protect a disk, you can only read from it, you can't change the information. If you ever need the diskette, you'll have a good copy of your system files and the virus-detection program. (An ounce of prevention is worth....)

Scanning for Viruses

If you suspect a virus, immediately exit all programs, including the DOS Shell. Boot your system with your startup diskette. At the DOS prompt, type **MSAV /A / C** and press **Enter**. (If you are connected to a network, type **MSAV /L /C**. This will limit scanning to local drives only.) The Anti-Virus Main Menu appears, as shown in Figure 16.1. All local drives are scanned and cleaned of any viruses found. After the scan is complete, press **F3** to exit. Whew! Close one.

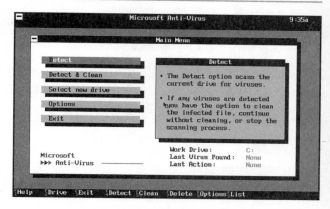

Figure 16.1 *Select scanning options from the Anti-Virus screen.*

If you prefer to control the virus scanning manually, type **MSAV** at the prompt. From the Anti-Virus main menu, select from among these options:

☞ If necessary, press **F2** or choose Select new drive to change the drive you want to check for viruses.

☞ Press **F8** or choose Options to change various scanning options, such as disabling the alarm sound and creating a report of the virus scan.

☞ Start the scan by selecting either Detect (**F4**) or Detect & Clean (**F5**). If you choose Detect, you will be able to select a course of action if an infected file is detected.

Can I Make My Computer Do Virus Scans Automatically at Startup?

To perform a scan of your hard disk every time you boot your computer, add **MSAV /N** to your

AUTOEXEC.BAT file. (Type **EDIT AUTOEXEC.BAT** at the command prompt, add the command, save the file, and then exit.) If you are attached to a network, use **MSAV /N /L** instead.

With one of these commands in place, your hard disk will be scanned automatically at startup. If any viruses are detected, a dialog box will appear that will offer several options for how to deal with the bug.

Using the MSAV command at startup will detect only viruses that are active at that time. To have ongoing protection, run VSafe. VSafe is a program that runs in the background as you perform your normal computer tasks. VSafe will warn you of changes to your files that might be caused by viruses. To start VSafe automatically every time you boot your computer, add VSAFE to your AUTOEXEC.BAT file.

Did you ever think that computing could be so dangerous? You have just learned how to detect and prevent viruses. In the next lesson, you will learn how to double your hard disk space and double your fun with DoubleSpace.

Lesson 17

Doubling Your Disk Space with DoubleSpace

What's a Compressed Drive?

Disk compression programs such as DoubleSpace can store more information on a disk because data is stored more densely than with MS-DOS alone. If you use DoubleSpace, your hard disk can increase its capacity by almost two times.

When you install DOS 6, your drives are still uncompressed. After you install DoubleSpace, your hard disk will consist of two sections, as shown in Figure 17.1. One section will remain uncompressed, to support the few programs and system files that cannot run on a compressed drive.

You can use a drive compressed with DoubleSpace the same way you use any regular drive; the only difference is that it will store more files than it normally would. Unbelievable? Too good to be true? The next section explains how its done.

> **Tip**
>
> **Check Those Utilities** If you use any third-party utilities, such as PC Tools or Norton Utilities, make sure that they are compatible with a DoubleSpace drive. If you're not sure, consult the manual or call the manufacturer before you run these programs.

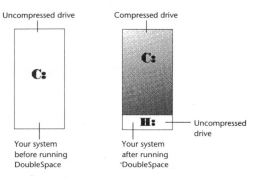

Figure 17.1   Before and after DoubleSpace installation.

How DoubleSpace Works

If you don't care about how DoubleSpace works, you can skip this part. But I'm going to explain it for those of you who are doubtful that this process can work. After DoubleSpace installation, your drive C is unaltered. But there is a humongous file that takes up most of it now. This huge file, called *DBLSPACE.000*, is your compressed drive. DOS assigns a drive letter to this file, so you can access your files from it.

Most Illogical   The DBLSPACE.000 file is not really a drive. DOS pretends that it is, so the files within it can be read normally. A drive that is not physically a drive is called a *logical drive*. (Go figure.)

All the files that were formerly on your hard disk are compressed into DBLSPACE.000, along with most of the free space remaining on the drive. A little bit of free space is left outside of DBLSPACE.000 (uncompressed) in case you need it.

Here's the tricky part. DOS knows that you expect all the files that were on C: before to be accessible from C: now. So it assigns the drive letter C to the *compressed* drive, and changes the name of the *real* drive C to something else (usually H: or I:). That way you can still do everything from the C: prompt like you did before you compressed your hard disk. Truly incredible!

I'm Convinced; Now How Do I Use DoubleSpace?

> **Tip**
>
> **There's No Looking Back** Once you compress a drive, you can shrink its size, but you can't reverse the compression process. If you try to do this by deleting the DBLSPACE.000 file, you'll lose everything that was on the compressed drive. As a safety precaution, do a full backup before running DoubleSpace (see Lesson 14).

To set up DoubleSpace, first exit all programs, including the DOS Shell. Change to the DOS directory by typing **CD\DOS** and pressing **Enter**. Start the DoubleSpace setup program by typing **DBLSPACE** and pressing **Enter**. To exit at any time, press **F3**.

Choose between *Custom* or *Express* setup. (Unless you are an experienced user, select **Express** setup.) A small section of your drive will remain uncompressed. If you want to change the default letter for the uncompressed drive, do it before pressing Enter.

A message will appear which tells you how long the compression process will take. This one-time process takes about one minute per megabyte. (This could take a while.) Press **C** to Continue (which will complete the compression process) or **Esc** to exit (which will stop it).

After the disk compression is finished, a summary will display, showing information on the compressed drive. Press **Enter**, and your system will restart with the compressed drive active.

Now That I Have a Compressed Drive, What Do I Do with It?

Work with your compressed drive as you would with any other drive. The compression process remains invisible to you, the user. You can access the DoubleSpace maintenance program by typing **DBLSPACE** at the DOS prompt. The maintenance program allows you to perform these compression functions:

- ☞ Increase the storage capacity of diskettes by compressing them.
- ☞ Adjust the size of your compressed drive.
- ☞ Display information about the compressed drive.
- ☞ Format a compressed drive.
- ☞ Defragment a compressed drive.

What Does Defragment Mean? When a file is placed on a drive, parts of the file may be split over different sections of the drive in order to make the most effective use of available space. On an uncompressed drive, fragmentation can cause a drop in speed when accessing files. *Defragmenting* a drive causes the parts of files that were split up to be placed together. Defragmenting a compressed drive may not affect speed as much as on an uncompressed drive, but it will usually result in additional space on the drive.

You are finished learning about DoubleSpace. (Or more correctly, I am finished talking about it.) Let's move on to a frank discussion of some things that I personally think are important for you to know.

Lesson 18

If You Never Learn Anything Else About DOS . . .

Basic Things I Think You Should Know

My dad made me take Calculus in high school because he thought it would be good for me to know. Now I wonder: how many people took Calculus years ago and have never *ever* seen a derivative since? I wouldn't be able to tell a derivative from a logarithm. Unlike Calculus, there are some things about DOS that you will be better off knowing. And, unlike Trigonometry, which I also had to take, these DOS things are practical things that you'll use later on. You might even use them every day like I do.

How to Change Your DOS Prompt

One of the things you might want to do is change your prompt. (I didn't say this stuff was hard, did I?) You can change it to basically whatever you want. The egotistical "Yes, Master" and the Al Bundyish "What the Heck Do You Want Now?" prompts inevitably appear on some people's screens. Geekier people know how to change the colors of their prompts and everything.

Because it would waste our time to discuss all the different things you can do with your prompt, I'm only going to tell you a few things. The command you use to change it is PROMPT. You can type the word **PROMPT**, then a space, and then enter whatever you want your prompt to say. If you want it to tell you the current directory and then display a greater than sign (this is a common and handy prompt) type **PROMPT**

PG. (The dollar signs and letters are codes DOS uses that represent things like directories, the date, symbols, and so on.)

If you want your computer to display your name, the current directory, and a greater than sign, type **PROMPT *your name* PG**. (And all you smart alecks who typed "your name" instead of filling in your own name aren't fooling me; I'm onto you guys.) Imagine the hours of fun you can have with this trick!

The Amazing DIR Command

One of the commands I probably use the most is DIR. This stands for *directory*, and you can use it to see the files in any directory. Not only that, but you can add all sorts of stuff to the end of DIR to make it do exactly what you want. (See the Command Reference that tells about all the stuff you can add on to the end of DIR.)

I usually add two things to the DIR command: the /P *switch* and some wild cards for the file names. What is a /P switch, you ask? Well, switches are things DOS uses to narrow down a command or to vary the command. It has a slash (called a *delimiter*) in front of it because when you type the slash, DOS knows you are adding something onto the command. (Make sure to use the forward slash, not the backslash.)

For example, if you type just plain **DIR** at the DOS prompt and press **Enter**, all your files start scrolling by at an incredibly rapid pace. That doesn't help at all because you can't read any of them. However, when you type **DIR /P**, you will be able to see your files one screen at a time (you got it, P stands for Page). You can press any key to go on to the next screen.

You can use wild cards to have DOS list specific files. If you want to see a list of all the files that start with S and have a .DOC extension, you would type

DIR S*.DOC. (The * wild card tells DOS that any character(s) could be there.) If you only want the files that are five digits long and start with S and have a .DOC extension, you would type DIR S????.DOC. The ? wild card tells DOS that it should only list files that have only one character in place of the question mark. For example, DIR S*.DOC would find SLIME.DOC, STUPID.DOC, and STINKY.DOC, but DIR S????.DOC would only find SLIME.DOC because it's the only one with four characters after the S.

Can I See a List of My Directories? If you want to list your directories, type **DIR *.** (with no extension). Since most directories don't (and shouldn't) have extensions, this command will list all the files without extensions—that is, your directories.

Are All DOS Things This Easy to Learn?

Let's not get our hopes up. I'm not finished with this very important stuff you need to learn, and as luck would have it, I saved the worst for last. Don't get all psyched out yet, though. This isn't as hard as, say, Calculus; it's just some of that really weird DOS technical stuff.

First of all, you might have heard some computer geeks tossing around terms like "AUTOEXEC.BAT file" and "CONFIG.SYS file." No? Well, if you hung around computer geeks, you would hear them talking about these files. These are DOS's startup files. You can put stuff in these files to tell DOS what you want it to do when it starts your computer. Geeks call it *configuration*.

When I first started using DOS, no one told me what these files were. People pronounce them just like they're spelled, so until someone tells you what the abbreviated form stands for, you're clueless. All I knew was that I should never, never touch or change these files or I would probably break my computer. (Which, by the way, is hooey. It is very hard to break a computer. However, it is true that you shouldn't edit your startup files without making backup copies first.)

In the first place, don't believe the hype. I'd bet that several of those people who are so casually throwing around "AUTOEXEC.BAT" and "CONFIG.SYS" don't *really* know what the things actually are. They're just trying to impress and intimidate you.

So Quit Stalling and Tell Me What AUTOEXEC.BAT Is

First of all, AUTOEXEC.BAT is a *batch* file. This accounts for the .BAT extension. Batch files are simply files that contain lists of DOS commands. When you run the batch file, DOS executes all the commands in the file. This is really handy because you can type one command to run the batch file instead of typing the twenty or so commands in the file one at a time.

This particular batch file is *AUTO*matically *EXEC*uted when you boot your computer. Your AUTOEXEC.BAT file should contain a line that lists your directories separated by semicolons. This is called a *path statement* and looks something like this:

PATH=C:\;C:\DOS;C:\WINDOWS;C:\WORD

If you have a path statement in your AUTOEXEC.BAT file, you won't have to change to a directory to use the commands contained in it. For example, if you have Windows and the directory is in your path statement, you can just type **win** at the DOS prompt, instead of switching to the Windows directory and typing win.

There are other types of things in your AUTOEXEC.BAT file, but the path is probably the only one you might need to worry about (PROMPT PG also is usually there). My AUTOEXEC.BAT file is shown in Figure 18.1.

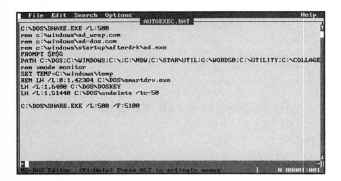

```
  File  Edit  Search  Options                                          Help
                                  AUTOEXEC.BAT
C:\DOS\SHARE.EXE /L:500
rem c:\windows\ad_wrap.com
rem c:\windows\ad-dos.com
rem c:\windows\startup\afterdrk\ad.exe
PROMPT $P$G
PATH C:\DOS;C:\WINDOWS;C:\;C:\WDW;C:\STAR\UTIL;C:\WORD50;C:\UTILITY;C:\COLLAGE
rem vmode monitor
SET TEMP=C:\windows\temp
REM LH /L:0;1,42304 C:\DOS\smartdrv.exe
LH /L:1,6400 C:\DOS\DOSKEY
LH /L:1,51440 C:\DOS\undelete /tc-50

C:\DOS\SHARE.EXE /L:500 /F:5100




MS-DOS Editor   <F1=Help> Press ALT to activate menus          N 00001:001
```

Figure 18.1   The AUTOEXEC.BAT file in all its glory.

What Is the Other One Good For?

Fortunately, you usually don't have to worry about CONFIG.SYS. This is the *CONFIG*uration file that you can use to change the default settings on your computer. The .SYS extension usually tells you that the file is a *device driver*, which is a program that tells your computer how to use various devices, like your mouse or your monitor. Only in CONFIG.SYS's case, it's the master of all device drivers. If you need a device driver loaded, you put a line naming it in your CONFIG.SYS file, and the driver will load every time you start your computer.

The commands in your CONFIG.SYS file cannot be run from the DOS prompt; they only can load at startup, and only through CONFIG.SYS. For example, you can set the number of files that can be opened in a program at one time, or you can tell your computer to use memory more efficiently. Unless you're really getting into some heavy computer-type stuff, the settings in your CONFIG.SYS file (which was automatically created when you installed DOS 5 or above) are probably fine. But if you're ever just dying to find out more about these commands and other weird DOS things, I recommend *The First Book of MS-DOS 6* by Joe Kraynak.

Tip

Mother May I? If you install a new program, the installation program may request permission to modify your CONFIG.SYS. Let it.

If you know what's good for you, you'll remember all the things you learned in this lesson. Guess what? There are no more lessons! I don't have anything else to tell you. It looks like it might be time for both of us to go home, put our feet up, and revel in our DOS wisdom.

Appendix A

Installing or Upgrading to DOS 6

Have a formatted disk (for drive A) ready. It will be used to create an Uninstall diskette, which can be used to return to your previous DOS version if you encounter problems. (If you are using double-density diskettes, have two diskettes ready.)

To install DOS 6 on your system:

1. Place the Startup diskette in its drive.
2. Type **A:** and press **Enter**.
3. Type **SETUP** and press **Enter**.
4. Follow the on-screen instructions. When requested, place one of the formatted diskettes in drive A, and the uninstall diskette will be created. Put this diskette in a safe place. (If you want to uninstall DOS 6 at some later time, place this diskette in Drive A and reboot.)
5. After all the DOS 6 files have been copied, remove the final setup diskette, and press **Enter**. Your system will reboot under DOS 6—and you're ready to go!

Appendix B

What's New in DOS 6?

This appendix briefly describes the new features and enhancements in DOS 6. See the appropriate lessons for more details.

AUTOEXEC.BAT and CONFIG.SYS

You can define several configuration files and select which one to boot with. You can bypass commands selectively in AUTOEXEC.BAT or CONFIG.SYS, or even boot your computer without them. To completely bypass the AUTOEXEC.BAT and CONFIG.SYS files (clean boot) press **F5** at startup. To bypass selected commands in either file, press **F8** at startup.

DELTREE

Use the DELTREE command to delete a directory and its subdirectories, *without having to remove its files.*

DoubleSpace

Allows you to compress a disk or diskette so that it will hold up to two times more data. Once DoubleSpace is installed, it works invisibly. See Lesson 17 for more details.

EMM386

Improvements allow EMM386.EXE to take better advantage of unused areas in upper memory. Programs are able to use either expanded or extended memory as needed, without changing your PC's configuration.

Help

On-line Help has been expanded to a complete, graphical, on-line reference to all commands.

Interlink

Provides the ability to link two computers together to transfer files, and so on.

MemMaker

MemMaker configures your PC automatically to take the best advantage of the memory you have. MemMaker moves device drivers, memory-resident programs, and even DOS out of conventional memory, providing more working memory for all of your programs.

MEM

MEM provides more details about your system's memory usage. Using the /P switch causes MEM to display information one screen at a time.

Microsoft Anti-Virus

DOS now comes with a complete and easy-to-use program for virus detection and removal, based on Central Points Anti-Virus. There is also an Anti-Virus for Windows. See Lesson 16 for more details.

Microsoft Defragmenter

Based on the Norton Utilities, the Defragmenter can reorganize the files on your PC to allow for faster disk access. If you are not using DoubleSpace, exit all programs (including the DOS Shell and Windows), then type this command to defragment your drive:

DEFRAG C:

> **Don't Defrag de Drive** Don't use DEFRAG on a DoubleSpace drive, a network drive, or a drive created by using the INTERLNK command. Also, don't use DEFRAG from a DOS Shell, such as Shell or Windows.
>
> If you have a DoubleSpace drive, use the DoubleSpace utility to defragment it. Select the **T**ools **D**efragment command to defragment a DoubleSpace drive.

MOVE

Move files and rename directories with this versatile command. See Lesson 9 for more information.

MSBACKUP

Replacing DOS's antiquated BACKUP program is MSBACKUP, a graphical backup and restore program based on Norton Backup. See Lesson 14 for more details. A version of MSBACKUP is also provided for Windows.

POWER

Makes better use of your laptop's power.

SMARTDrive

Improvements in writing and reading information allows SMARTDrive to make the best use of system resources.

UNDELETE

Provides better tracking and easier recovery of deleted files. There is now an UNDELETE for Windows. See Lesson 11 for more details.

Appendix C

DOS Is at Your Command

A Command Reference for Those of Us Who Prefer to Work at the DOS Prompt

This section briefly describes the DOS commands used most often while at the DOS prompt. For more information about a particular command, type HELP *command* at the prompt. If you're not sure how to enter DOS commands at the prompt, or how to read DOS syntax, refer to DOS' on-line help for more information.

CD (CHDIR)

Displays or changes the active directory.

> **CD [d:][path]**
> **Example:** CD\WORD

CHKDSK

Displays available disk and memory space, and (optional) corrects disk errors.

> **CHKDSK [d:] [/F]**
> **Switches:**
>
> /F   Causes CHKDSK to fix any errors it finds.
> **Example:** CHKDSK C: /F

CLS

Clears your screen. A handy command for when people sneak up behind you and you don't want them to see what you've been doing.

CLS

COPY

Copies files to a directory or disk.

COPY   [d:][path]source.ext
               [d:][path][destination.ext]

Example: COPY C:\AUTOEXEC.BAT A:

DBLSPACE

Accesses the DoubleSpace program which is used to compress a drive or a diskette. Can also be used to mount a compressed diskette for use.

DBLSPACE [/MOUNT drive:]

Example: DBLSPACE or DBLSPACE /MOUNT A:

DEL

Deletes files.

DEL [d:][path]filename.ext [/P]

Switches:

/P   Asks for confirmation before deleting a file.

Example: DEL *.* /P

DELTREE

Deletes a directory and its subdirectories.

DELTREE [/Y][d:]path

Switches:

/Y   Deletes the directory tree without first prompting you to confirm.

Example: DELTREE C:\WORD\BUNK

DIR

Lists files in the specified directory. If you remember only one of the switches, remember the /P switch.

**DIR [d:][path][filename.ext]
[/P][/W][/A:attributes][/O:sortorder]
[/S][/B][/L][/C][/CH]**

Switches:

/P   Lists files one screen at time.

/W   Lists files across the screen.

/A   Lists files with selected attributes.

/O   Lists files in the selected order.

/S   Lists files in subdirectories, too.

/B   Lists files with no heading.

/L   Lists files in lowercase.

/C   Displays disk compression information, using a default 8K cluster size.

/CH   Displays disk compression information, using the cluster size of the host computer.

Example: DIR /P

DISKCOPY

Copies a diskette.

DISKCOPY sourcedisk: destinationdisk:
Example: DISKCOPY A: A:

DOSSHELL

Starts the DOS Shell. (Hold it up to your ear and you can hear the ocean!)

DOSSHELL

EDIT

Starts the DOS Editor and (optional) loads a file to edit.

EDIT [d:][path][filename.ext]

Example: EDIT C:\AUTOEXEC.BAT

EXIT

Returns you to the DOS Shell from the DOS command prompt.

EXIT

FORMAT

Prepares a diskette for use.

FORMAT d: [/S][/F:size][/Q][/U][V:label][/B]
Switches:

/S   Creates a bootable diskette.

/F   Formats to the specified size.

/Q   Performs a quick format.

/U   Performs an unconditional format.

/V   Adds a volume label to the formatted disk.

/B   Allocates space for system files, but does not copy them.

Example: FORMAT A:

HELP

Accesses the DOS help system.

HELP [command]

MAIL

Accesses the Microsoft Mail electronic mail system. (This command would be really impressive if it made your computer go down to the Post Office and mail your letters.)

MAIL

MD (MKDIR)

Creates a directory.

MD [d:]path
Example: MD C:\WORD\DOCS

MEM

Displays available memory.

MEM [/P][/C]
Switches:

/P   Displays one screenful at a time.

/C   Displays the programs in memory.

Example: MEM /P /C

MEMMAKER

Runs MemMaker, a program which automatically configures your system for best memory usage.

MEMMAKER

MOVE

Moves files to the location you specify. Also used to rename directories.

MOVE [d:][originalpath]filename.ext [d:]destinationpath[filename.ext]

Example: MOVE C:\OLDSUB C:\NEWSUB or

MOVE C:\MKTG\JFSALES.DOC

D:\SALES\DSSALES.DOC

MSAV

Runs Microsoft Anti-Virus, which checks the indicated drives for existing viruses, and optionally removes them, like a surgeon.

MSAV [d:] [/C] [/A] [/L] [/N]

Switches:

/C   Removes any viruses it finds.

/A   Scans all drives but A: and B:.

/L   Scans only local drives, not network drives.

/N   Scans for viruses while not displaying the normal   interface. Use this switch at startup.

Example: MSAV /A /C

MSBACKUP

Starts MS Backup, which you can use to back up or restore your hard disk or selected directories or files.

MSBACKUP

PROMPT

Customizes the DOS prompt.

PROMPT PGDT[text]

Options:

$P	Displays current directory path.
$G	Displays the greater-than sign.
$D	Displays the current date.
$T	Displays the current time.
text	Displays the indicated text.

Example: PROMPT $P *Enter your command here*$G

RD (RMDIR)

Removes a directory if it's empty of files.

RD [d:]path

Example: RD \PROGRAMS\JUNK

REN

Renames a file.

REN [d:][path]original.ext [d:][path]new.ext

Example: REN OLDFILE.DOC NEWFILE.DOC

TREE

Tall vegetation with a trunk and branches. Okay, okay, this kind of tree displays directory paths.

TREE [d:][path][/F][/A]

Switches:

/F   Lists files in each directory.

/A   Produces an alternate character for the lines
      that link subdirectories. Use for printer out-
      put.

Example: TREE /F

TYPE

Displays the contents of a file. (Don't try to use this
command with program files; you won't be able to
read any of the junk that appears on the screen and the
computer will probably beep at you.)

TYPE [d:][path]filename.ext [¦MORE]

Options:

¦MORE Using the MORE filter with the TREE
command will cause the output to display one
screen at a time.

Example: TYPE C:\AUTOEXEC.BAT ¦MORE

UNDELETE

Restores deleted files. Also used to establish a delete
file tracking system.

**UNDELETE [d:][path][/LIST][/DT][/DS][/DOS]
[/ALL][/PURGE][/LOAD][/UNLOAD][/STATUS]
[/S[drive]][/T[drive]]**

Switches:

/LIST	Lists all files that can be undeleted.
/DT	Uses the tracking file when undeleting.
/DS	Uses the delete sentry file when undeleting.
/DOS	Uses DOS when undeleting.
/ALL	Undeletes without prompting.

/PURGE	Purges the DELETE SENTRY directory.
/LOAD	Loads UNDELETE.
/UNLOAD	Unloads UNDELETE.
/STATUS	Displays status on UNDELETE.
/S	Enables delete sentry.
/T	Enables delete tracking.

Example: UNDELETE \PROGRAMS\JUNK /LIST

UNFORMAT

Unformats a diskette.

UNFORMAT d: [/P][/L][/TEST]

Switches:

/P	Sends output to printer.
/L	Lists files and directories found on disk.
/TEST	Verifies that an UNFORMAT can be done, but doesn't do it.

Example: UNFORMAT A: /TEST

VER

Displays the current DOS version.

VER

VOL

Displays (and allows you to change) the volume label of a disk.

VOL [d:]

VSAFE

Loads a memory resident anti-virus program that detects viruses as you work.

VSAFE

Appendix D

Common DOS Error Messages

This appendix lists the everyday DOS error messages you might encounter while working with your computer, what they mean, and it lets you in on how to fix them.

Abort, Retry, Ignore, Fail?

A device error has occurred, such as no disk in your drive or a printer being out of paper. Fix the problem and press R for Retry, or press A to give up.

Access Denied

Sounds serious, huh? A file you are trying to modify is a read-only file. Change the file's attributes with ATTRIB, then try again. You'll also get this error message if you're trying to treat a directory as a file.

ANSI.SYS must be installed to perform requested function

The program you are trying to run requires ANSI.SYS. Add the following line to your CONFIG.SYS file: DEVICE=C:\DOS\ANSI.SYS. Reboot (Ctrl+Alt+Del) and try again.

Bad command or file name

This message can be caused by several things. The command you typed is not spelled right, does not exist, or DOS can't find it in the current directory or path. Try again. If it doesn't work, change to the appropriate directory (CD) and try again. If it still doesn't work, check to make sure you have the right name for the program (use DIR).

Bad or missing Command Interpreter

The disk you are booting from does not contain a valid COMMAND.COM file, which it needs to run. Insert a bootable floppy disk into the A: drive and restart your computer. (A bootable disk contains three files: COMMAND.COM, IO.SYS, and MSDOS.SYS. The latter two are hidden files.)

Cannot execute x

See "Error in EXE file."

Cannot make directory entry

Oops, it's full. Your disk's root directory contains the maximum entries it can hold, so there is no room for the file or directory you are trying to make. Solution: delete some files or directories from the root directory and then try again.

Current drive is no longer valid

This message means that the active drive does not have a usable disk in it, and you need to pick a different drive to be active (or find a usable disk). To change drives, type a new drive letter and a colon (C:) and press Enter.

Data error reading drive x
Abort, Retry, Fail?

DOS is telling you it can't read a file on your disk. The disk probably has a bad spot, like a banana. Press R to try again. Try several times. If it still doesn't work, press A to give up.

Directory already exists

Hey, you're trying to create a directory with the same name as an existing directory. Just choose another name and try again.

Disk boot failure

This means DOS is having a difficult time loading itself at startup. Restart your comptuer (Ctrl+Alt+Del) and try again. If the message returns, turn off the computer's power, wait 30 seconds, and try again. Error message still shows up? Boot from a floppy disk, then use SYS to transfer DOS system files onto your hard disk.

Disk unsuitable for system disk

You are trying to make a system (bootable) disk out of a disk that is not suitable for it. Try a different disk.

Divide overflow

Yikes! You're running a poorly-written or defective program. Reboot and try again. If that doesn't help, return your program and get a refund!

Drive types or diskette types not compatible
Copy process ended
Copy another diskette (Y/N)?

You're trying to use DISKCOPY with disks that are not the same. DISKCOPY only works with the same size and same density diskettes. Otherwise, you must use COPU or XCOPY.

Duplicate file name or file not found

You're renaming a file with a name that already exists. Try a different name.

Error in EXE file

There's a problem with the program file you are trying to run. It's been damaged or tampered with. Recopy the file from the original disk it came on.

Error in loading operating system

The area on disk where your DOS startup files are kept may be damaged. Reboot and try again. If it doesn't go away, boot from a floppy disk, and try changing to the C: drive. If you can change to the C: drive, recopy the system files to your hard drive with SYS C:. If you can't change to C:, you probably have a hard disk problem and need to contact your dealer.

Execute failure

When you see this message, either the program file is damaged, or you don't have enough files available. Try the solution listed under "Error in EXE file". If that doesn't work, increase the number on the FILES= line in your CONFIG.SYS file.

Fail on INT 24

An unrecognized error has occurred. The most common cause for this is repeatedly choosing F for Fail when offered the choices of "Abort, Retry, Fail." Take care of the problem that caused the "Abort, Retry, Fail" message, then try again.

File allocation table bad, drive x
Abort, Retry, Fail?

Ooh, the disk you're trying to use is messed up. Try choosing R for Retry several times. If it doesn't go away, choose A for Abort. Copy all the data you can salvage off the disk, and throw the disk away.

If the message occured on a hard drive, back up all the files you can, then reformat the disk (FORMAT). This is a drastic step, so you may want to try a disk recovery program like Norton Utilities first.

File cannot be copied onto itself

Guess what? You forgot to specify a destination when copying a file with COPY. Retype the command, make sure you put in a destination.

File Creation Error

You're trying to create a file with the same name as an existing hidden file or directory. Or, the root directory on your disk is full. Check to make sure the name is unique. If it turns out your root directory is full, delete some files and try again. (Disks vary as to how many files their root directories can hold. For a floppy, it's somewhere around a 100, for a hard disk drive, it's around 500.)

File is READ-ONLY

You're trying to write over a read-only file. Use ATTRIB to change the file's attributes, then try again.

File not found

DOS is telling you that whatever file you're trying to work with doesn't exist by that name, or it's in a different location. Check the name and try again. (This message also shows up when you type DEL *.* in an already-empty directory.)

General failure (reading or writing) drive x Abort, Retry, Fail?

Either the disk you're using has some bad spots, or it's unformatted. Choose R a couple of times, or give up by pressing A. If the disk has important stuff on it, use a disk recovery program like Norton Utilities. Otherwise, reformat the disk.

Help not available for this command

You'll see this message in DOS version 5. It means that DOS can't help you with whatever command you've asked for help with.

Incorrect DOS version

The command you're trying to use does not work with the version of DOS that you have. If the command appears in an application program, it may require an earlier version of DOS. Sometimes you can trick the program by using SETVER.

Insufficient disk space

Your disk is full. Delete some files and try again, or use a different disk.

Insufficient memory

Yowsa! Your computer doesn't have enough free memory to run the program. Try eliminating some of the memory-resident programs from your AUTOEXEC.BAT and some of the infrequently-needed drivers from your CONFIG.SYS, then reboot and try again.

Internal stack overflow
System halted

Don't panic. If this error occurs once, reboot and ignore it. If it occurs frequently, increase the available stacks with the STACKS= command in your CONFIG.SYS.

Invalid characters in volume label

You're trying to label a disk using invalid characters. Don't use *?/\|.,;:+=[].

Invalid COMMAND.COM

Uh-oh. Your COMMAND.COM file has been damaged. Reboot your computer using a bootable floppy disk (such as your original DOS diskette), then recopy COMMAND.COM from that disk.

Invalid date

You've typed in the date wrong when DOS asked for it. Try again using valid characters.

Invalid directory

This time, you've tried to change to a directory that doesn't exist. Check your typing and try again.

Invalid drive in search path

One of your entries in your PATH statement has an invalid disk drive name. Either it doesn't exist, or it may have been hidden temporarily by a SUBST or

JOIN command. Edit your PATH command in AUTOEXEC.BAT to correct the error.

Invalid drive specification

You've typed the wrong letter when specifying a drive. Check your typing and try again.

Invalid file name or file not found

This message occurs when you try to use wildcard characters with the TYPE command. That's a no-no. You can't use ? or * with TYPE.

Invalid media or Track 0 Bad - disk unusable
Format terminated
Format another (Y/N)?

Either you're trying to format a disk to be a capacity it wasn't able to be, or the diskette is defective. Use a different disk.

Invalid parameter specifications

At least one of the parameters you've typed in for a command is not correct. Review the syntax for the command you are trying to use. (This message also appears as Incorrect parameter, or Invalid parameter.)

Invalid path, not directory, or directory not empty

You're trying to remove a current directory that isn't empty or doesn't exist. Or you might be trying to delete a file using the RD command. A directory must be empty before you can remove it with RD. Use DELTREE to remove a directory and delete its files at the same time.

Invalid switch

You're using a switch inappropriately with a DOS command. Check it and try again.

Memory allocation error
Cannot load MS-DOS, system halted

Woah! A program you've been running has messed up DOS's recollection of its available memory. Reboot your system and try again. If the problem persists, boot from a floppy disk, then use SYS to recopy the system files to your hard disk.

No Path

You typed PATH to see what your path is set to, but no path has been specified. Type PATH= and then the drive and directories you want to include in the path. (If you put the PATH= line in your AUTOEXEC.BAT file, you won't have to type it every time.)

No room for system on destination disk

You're trying to use SYS to make a disk bootable, but the disk does not have room in the right places for the system files. System files are particular about where they're located on the disk. Delete all the files from the disk and try again.

Non-System disk or disk error
Replace and strike any key when ready

You're booting from an unbootable disk! You can make a disk bootable by using SYS. Remove the disk and replace with a different one, or leave the drive empty if you want to reboot from your hard disk.

Not ready reading drive x
Abort, Retry, Fail?

Wake up! You're drive's not ready. You probably left the door open or forgot to put a disk in it. Correct the problem and press R for Retry.

Packed file is corrupt

Not really. Type LOADFIX, a space, and then the regular command you were trying to use.

Parameter format not correct

You're not using the correct parameters for the command you're issuing. Review the parameters for that command and try again.

Printer out of paper error
writing device PRN
Abort, Retry, Ignore, Fail?

Okay, just put some more paper in your printer and press R for Retry.

Program too big to fit in memory

DOS thinks it doesn't have enough room in RAM for the program. Reboot and try again. Sometimes DOS is just mistaken. (Imagine that?) If this doesn't solve the problem you may actually not have enough memory, so check the program's requirements.

Read fault error reading drive x
Abort, Retry, Fail?

Your PC can't read data from the designated drive. Press R for Retry. If that doesn't work, try removing and reinserting the disk. If that still doesn't work, your disk may be unusable.

Required parameter missing

You left out a parameter the command needs. Review your typing and try again.

Sector not found
Abort, Retry, Fail?

DOS can't read a sector on your disk. The disk might be damaged, or your drive might be messed up. Try R for Retry. If that doesn't work, choose A to give up. Try a different disk to see if the problem was the disk or drive.

If the problem turns out to be your hard drive, contact your dealer. There may be something wrong with your hard disk controller or your system motherboard.

Seek error
Abort, Retry, Fail?

DOS can't find the requested file on your disk. Remove and reinsert, press R to try again. If the problem persists with different disks you use, you might have a tracking problem with your drive. Time to call your dealer.

Sharing violation
Abort, Retry, Fail?

You're running a program that requires SHARE.EXE to be loaded. Exit to the DOS prompt, type SHARE, and try again.

TARGET diskette bad or incompatible

You're duplicating a disk with DISKCOPY and the target disk is not the same type as your source disk. Get an appropriate disk and try again.

Track 0 bad diskette unsuable

There are bad sectors in the disk that prevent it from being formatted. Throw it away!

Too many parameters

Oops, you've typed in too many commands on a line. Try again, typing only one command at a time.

Unable to write BOOT

You're formatting a disk that has defects where the system files are written. Throw it away!

Unrecognized command in CONFIG.SYS
Error in CONFIG.SYS line x

DOS doesn't understand a line in your CONFIG.SYS file. Edit the line, correct the typo, then reboot your system.

WARNING ALL DATA ON NON-REMOVABLE DISK DRIVE X: WILL BE LOST!
Proceed with format (Y/N)?

Aaahhh! You specified a hard disk with the FORMAT command. If you really meant to, press Y to proceed to delete all data on that drive. If you didn't mean to, press N.

Write failure, diskette unusable

This disk can't be made into a system disk (with SYS). Discard it.

Write fault error writing device PRN

Hey! This means turn your printer on.

Write fault error writing drive x
Abort, Retry, Fail?

DOS can't write data to the specified disk. Reinsert the disk and try again. If it still doesn't work, get rid of the disk.

Write protect error writing drive x
Abort, Retry, Fail?

The disk you are trying to write to is write-protected. Remove the write-protection from the disk, then select R for Retry. (The write protection is a black piece of tape covering the notch on the side of a 5.25-inch disk. It's a tiny black square that reveals a hole on a 3.5-inch disk.)

Index

J-K

L

Other Idiot-Proof Books from Alpha!

If you enjoyed this Complete Idiot's Pocket Guide, then you may want to check out the rest!

Complete Idiot's Pocket Guides

The Complete Idiot's
Pocket Guide to DOS 6
ISBN: 1-56761-303-9
Softbound, $5.99 USA

The Complete Idiot's
Pocket Guide to Windows
(version 3.1)
ISBN: 1-56761-302-0
Softbound, $5.99 USA

The Complete Idiot's
Pocket Guide to
WordPerfect 6
ISBN: 1-56761-300-4
Softbound, $5.99 USA

The Complete Idiot's
Pocket Guide to Word for
Windows (version 2)
ISBN: 1-56761-301-2
Softbound, $5.99 USA

If you can't find these books at your local computer book retailer, call this toll-free number for more information! 1-800-428-5331

Cheaper Than Therapy!

Complete Idiot's Guides

Learn everything you need to know about computers from our best-selling series!

The Complete Idiot's Guide to Windows
ISBN: 1-56761-175-3
Softbound, $14.95 USA

The Complete Idiot's Guide to DOS
ISBN: 1-56761-169-9
Softbound, $14.95 USA

The Complete Idiot's Guide to PCs
ISBN: 1-56761-168-0
Softbound, $14.95 USA

The Complete Idiot's Guide to Word for Windows
ISBN: 1-56761-174-5
Softbound, $14.95 USA

The Complete Idiot's Guide to WordPerfect
ISBN: 1-56761-187-7
Softbound, $14.95 USA

The Complete Idiot's Guide to Computer Terms
ISBN: 1-56761-266-0
Softbound, $9.95 USA

The Complete Idiot's Guide to 1-2-3
Coming in August 1993
ISBN: 1-56761-285-7
Softbound, $14.95 USA

The Complete Idiot's Guide to VCRs
Coming in September 1993
ISBN: 1-56761-294-6
Softbound, $9.95 USA

If you can't find these books at your local computer book retailer, call this toll-free number for more information! 1-800-428-5331